T0368919

Ladybird Readers

What Do You Like?

To access the audio and digital versions
of this book:

1 Go to www.ladybirdeducation.co.uk
2 Click "Unlock book"
3 Enter the code below

KpJDkfVpVH

Notes to teachers, parents, and carers

The *Ladybird Readers* Beginner level helps young language learners to become familiar with key conversational phrases in English. The language introduced has clear real-life applications, giving children the tools to hold their first conversations in English.

This book focuses on asking and answering the question "What do you like?" and provides practice of vocabulary for hobbies in English.

There are some activities to do in this book. They will help children practice these skills:

 Speaking    Listening*   Reading

*To complete these activities, listen to the audio downloads available at **www.ladybirdeducation.co.uk**

Series Editor: Sorrel Pitts
Chants by Sorrel Pitts

LADYBIRD BOOKS

UK | USA | Canada | Ireland | Australia
India | New Zealand | South Africa

Ladybird Books is part of the Penguin Random House group of companies
whose addresses can be found at global.penguinrandomhouse.com.
www.penguin.co.uk   www.puffin.co.uk   www.ladybird.co.uk

Penguin
Random House
UK

Text inspired by *Friends* by Eric Carle, first published in Great Britain by Puffin Books, 2013
This version first published by Ladybird Books 2024
001

Text and illustrations copyright © Penguin Random House LLC, 2013
Adapted text and artwork copyright © 2024 by Penguin Random House LLC
The moral right of the original author/illustrator has been asserted

ERIC CARLE's name and signature logotype and the World of Eric Carle logo are trademarks of Penguin Random House LLC.
This edition published by arrangement with World of Eric Carle, an imprint of Penguin Young Readers Group, a division of Penguin Random House LLC.
All rights reserved including the right of reproduction in whole or in part in any form.
To find out more about Eric Carle and his books, please visit eric-carle.com. To learn about The Eric Carle Museum of Picture Book Art, please visit carlemuseum.org.

Printed in China

The authorized representative in the EEA is Penguin Random House Ireland, Morrison Chambers, 32 Nassau Street, Dublin D02 YH68

A CIP catalogue record for this book is available from the British Library

ISBN: 978–0–241–58766–9

All correspondence to:
Ladybird Books
Penguin Random House Children's
One Embassy Gardens, 8 Viaduct Gardens, London SW11 7BW

MIX
Paper | Supporting
responsible forestry
FSC® C018179

What Do You Like?

Inspired by
Friends
by Eric Carle

"What do you like?"
says the boy.

"I like running,"
says the girl.

"What do you like?"
says the girl.

"I like dancing,"
says the boy.

"What do you like?"
says the boy.

"I like games,"
says the girl.

"What do you like?"
says the girl.

"I like flowers,"
says the boy.

"What do you like?"
says the boy.

"I like my friends,"
says the girl.

Your turn!

1   Talk with a friend. ●

What does the girl like?

She likes running!

What does the boy like?

He likes dancing!

2 **Listen. Put a** ✓ **by the correct words.**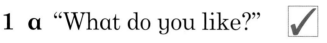

    1 a "What do you like?" ✓

       b "I like my friends." ☐

    2 a "I like dancing." ☐

       b "I like running." ☐

    3 a "I like games." ☐

       b "I like flowers." ☐

    4 a "I like my friends." ☐

       b "I like flowers." ☐

3 Read and clap!

I like running,
I like dancing,
I like playing games.
I like flowers,
Red flowers,
Be my friend today!

Friends like running,
Friends like dancing,
Friends like playing games.
Friends like flowers,
Red flowers,
We are friends. Let's play!